W9-CBC-403

Goliath Beetle

One of the World's Heaviest Insects

by Mary Packard

Consultant: Cameron R. Campbell
Coleopterist

PUBLISHING

New York, New York

Credits

Cover, ©Dorling Kindersley/Getty Images; 2–3, ©Sinclair Stammers/Photo Researchers; 4, Kathrin Ayer; 4–5, ©Bob Jensen/Photo Researchers; 6, ©Piotr Naskrecki/Minden Pictures; 7BKG, ©Piotr Naskrecki/Minden Pictures; 8–9, ©Dennis Sheridan/David Liebman; 10–11, ©Cameron Campbell; 12 (inset), ©Michael & Christine Denis-Huot/BIOS/Peter Arnold; 12–13, ©Dennis Sheridan/David Liebman; 14, ©Simon Trevor/Bruce Coleman; 15, ©Laurent Conchon/BIOS/Peter Arnold; 16, ©Cameron Campbell; 17, ©Cameron Campbell; 18, ©Cameron Campbell; 19, ©Cameron Campbell; 20 (inset), ©Ed Degginger/Animals Animals Earth Scenes; 20–21, ©Peter Payne/UNEP/Peter Arnold; 22L, ©George Bernard/NHPA; 22C, ©Pete Oxford/Minden Pictures; 22R, ©Mark Moffett/Minden Pictures; 23TR, ©Charlotte Thege/Das Fotoarchiv/Peter Arnold; 23BL, ©Dennis Sheridan/David Liebman; 23BR, ©Rick Sherwin/Oxford Scientific; 23BKG, ©Dennis Sheridan/David Liebman.

Publisher: Kenn Goin
Project Editor: Lisa Wiseman
Editorial Development: Nancy Hall, Inc.
Creative Director: Spencer Brinker
Photo Researcher: Carousel Research, Inc.: Mary Teresa Giancoli
Design: Otto Carbajal

Library of Congress Cataloging-in-Publication Data

Packard, Mary.
 Goliath beetle : one of the world's heaviest insects / by Mary Packard.
    p. cm. —(SuperSized!)
 Includes bibliographical references and index.
 ISBN-13: 978-1-59716-388-0 (lib. bdg.)
 ISBN-10: 1-59716-388-0 (lib. bdg.)
 1. Goliath beetles—Juvenile literature. I. Title.

QL596.S3P26 2007
595.76—dc22

                          2006034402

For more information, write to Bearport Publishing Company, Inc., 101 Fifth Avenue, Suite 6R, New York, New York 10003. Printed in the United States of America.

10 9 8 7 6 5 4 3 2 1

Contents

A Big Beetle

The Goliath beetle is one of the heaviest insects in the world.

A Goliath beetle weighs about the same as a chick.

A Goliath beetle can weigh up to 1.8 ounces (51 g). It can grow up to 4.3 inches (11 cm) long.

At Home in Africa

Goliath beetles are found only in Africa.

The heaviest Goliath beetles live in **rain forests** near the **equator**.

Beetles have been around for millions of years. They were even alive during the time of the dinosaurs.

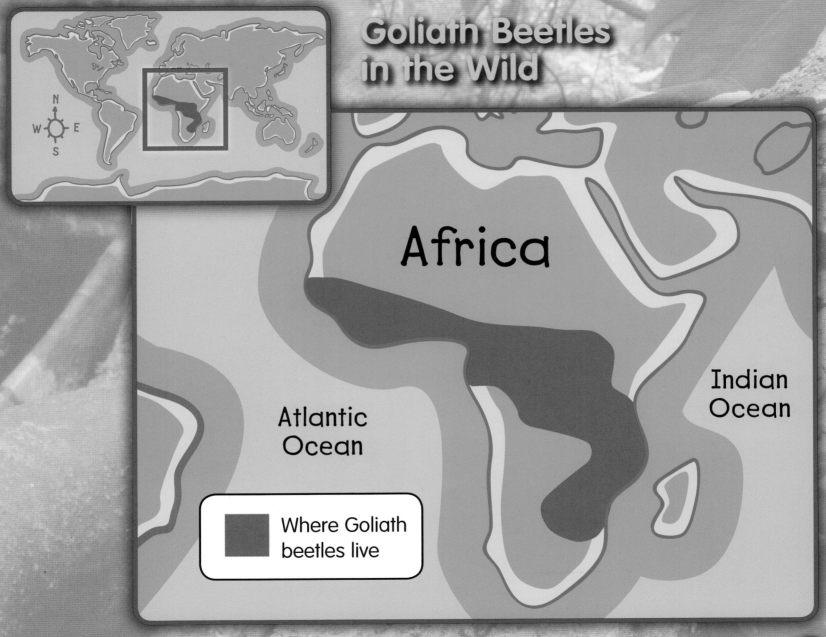

Goliath Beetles in the Wild

Africa

Atlantic Ocean

Indian Ocean

Where Goliath beetles live

Wings for Flying

A Goliath beetle has two pairs of wings.

One pair is for flying.

These flying wings are strong enough to lift the beetle's heavy body.

A Goliath beetle's flying wings are 8 inches (20 cm) long from tip to tip.

flying
wing

Two More Wings

The Goliath beetle's second pair of wings is very hard.

These outer wings cover and protect the beetle's flying wings.

The Goliath beetle spreads both sets of wings when it flies. Yet it flaps only its flying wings.

outer wings

Hide and Seek

Goliath beetles have patterns on their backs.

The beetles' dark colors and patterns match many plants.

They let the big beetles blend in with the rain forest.

Animals that want to eat these beetles can't easily find them.

Large birds and **genets** eat Goliath beetles.

genet

How Sweet!

Adult Goliath beetles eat sweet foods such as fruit.

They also climb trees to feed on sap.

A Goliath beetle has sharp claws to help it climb trees.

claws

Beetle Babies

Female Goliath beetles lay their eggs in dead tree trunks.

After two weeks, the eggs hatch into **grubs**.

The hungry grubs eat the rotten wood.

They eat dead plants, too.

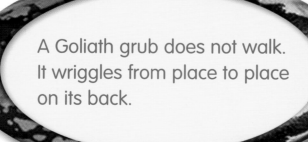

A Goliath grub does not walk. It wriggles from place to place on its back.

eggs

grub

A Special Case

When a grub is big enough, it makes itself a case.

It lives in the case for a few months.

When it comes out, it is a giant Goliath beetle.

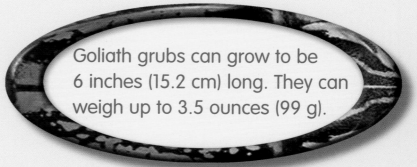

Goliath grubs can grow to be 6 inches (15.2 cm) long. They can weigh up to 3.5 ounces (99 g).

grub case

Clean-up Crew

By eating dead plants, Goliath grubs keep the rain forest clean.

The Goliath beetle is not only one of the heaviest insects in the world.

It is also one of our most helpful insects.

Adult Goliath beetles live for only a few months.

More Heavy Insects

Goliath beetles belong to a group of animals called insects. All insects have six legs and a body that is divided into three parts. Most insects hatch from eggs. Though almost all insects have wings, some do not.

Here are three more heavy insects.

Giant Burrowing Cockroach

The giant burrowing cockroach can weigh up to 1.2 ounces (34 g).

Madagascar Hissing Cockroach

The Madagascar hissing cockroach can weigh up to 1 ounce (28.3 g).

Giant Weta

The giant weta is a kind of cricket. It can weigh up to 0.7 ounces (19.8 g).

Goliath Beetle:
1.8 ounces/51 g

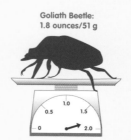

Giant Burrowing Cockroach:
1.2 ounces/34 g

Madagascar Hissing Cockroach:
1 ounce/28.3 g

Giant Weta:
0.7 ounces/19.8 g

Glossary

equator
(i-KWAY-tur)
an imaginary line halfway between the North and South Poles that runs around the middle of Earth

grubs
(GRUHBZ)
young beetles that look like worms

genets (JEN-its)
catlike, spotted animals with tails that are as long as their bodies

rain forests
(RAYN FOR-ists)
large areas of land covered with trees and plants, where lots of rain falls

Index

Read More

Facklam, Margery. *The Big Bug Book.* New York: Little, Brown & Company (1998).

Penner, Lucille Recht. *Monster Bugs.* New York: Random House Books for Young Readers (1996).

Learn More Online

To learn more about Goliath beetles, visit **www.bearportpublishing.com/SuperSized**